Sounds I Cannot Hear Clearly Anymore Add Up to the Sum of Silence

MARTIN WILLITTS JR.

Bainbridge Island Press

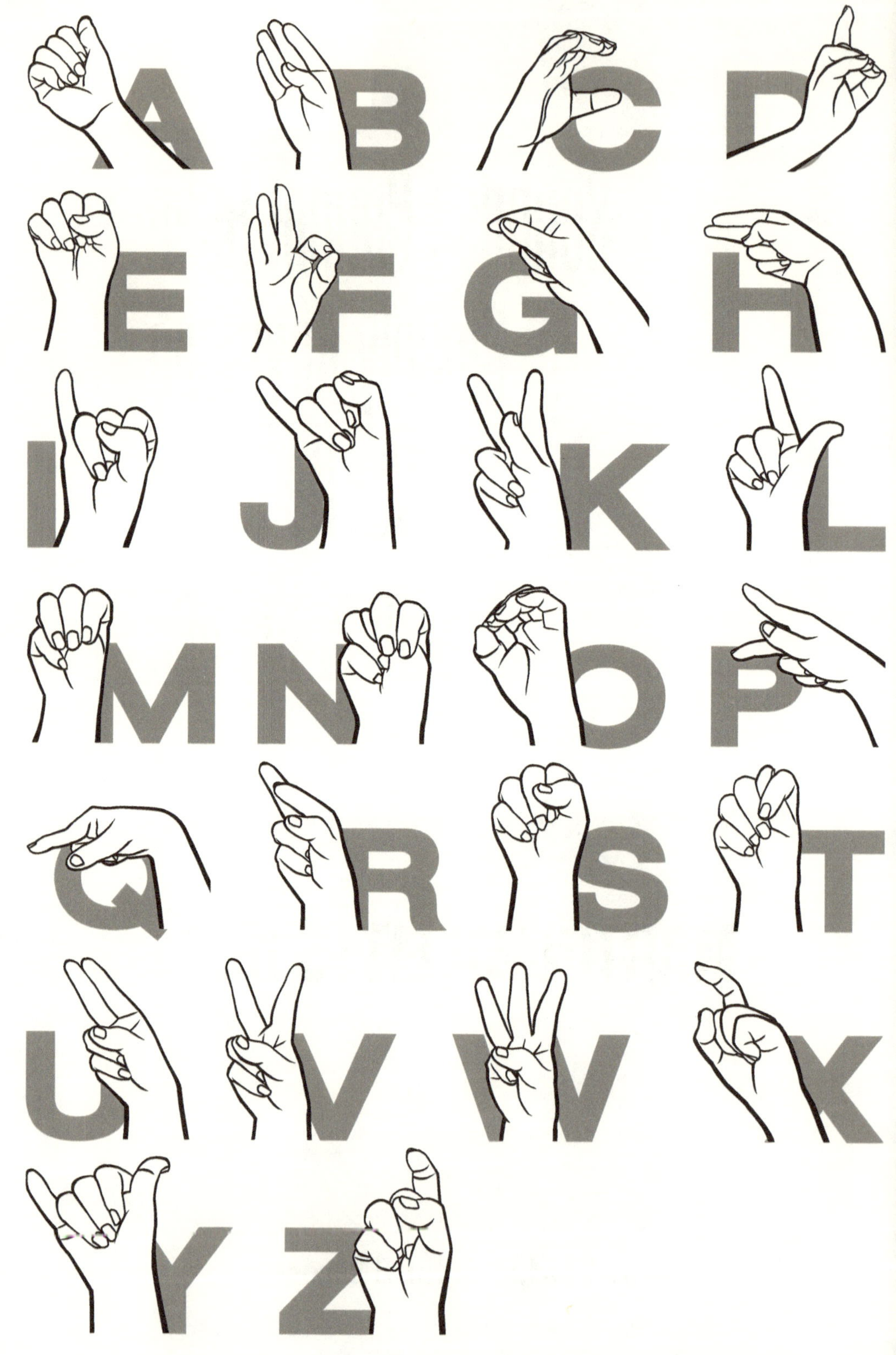

A
B
C
D
E
F
G
H
I
J
K
L
M
N
O
P
Q
R
S
T
U
V
W
X
Y
Z

POETRY

SOUNDS I CANNOT HEAR CLEARLY ANYMORE Add Up to the Sum of Silence

MARTIN WILLITTS JR.

Bainbridge Island Press

Bainbridge Island, WA

Sounds I Cannot Hear Clearly Anymore
Add Up to the Sum of Silence
by Martin Willitts Jr.
Copyright © 2026
All rights reserved

Published in 2026 by Bainbridge Island Press
Bainbridge Island, WA
https://bainbridgeisland.press

Printed in the United States of America

ISBN: 978-1-961451-14-8
Library of Congress Control Number: 2026938471

Editor: Tamarah Rockwood
Cover & Book Design: Ben Rockwood

9 8 7 6 5 4 3 2 1

Dedicated to the hearing impaired,

deaf community, and

all people who use sign language.

Contents

I.

II.

III.

IV.

Sounds I Cannot Hear Clearly Anymore Add Up to the Sum of Silence

I.

Sounds I Cannot Hear Clearly Anymore Add Up to the Sum of Silence

Consider ears that cannot hear
small sounds within silence of a forest,

hush-break when a rabbit squirms from sight
trying to avoid fox's sharp ears, teeth,

or a butterfly on milkweed,
or sound of an ocean still trapped

in a conch shell, or when trudging
uphill through brambles and branches.

I mishear words. Consider how language breaks:
I stammer to hear what cannot.

Blankness of my stare should be a clue.
Never let it be said that clarity has no value.

If I press my ear to heartbeat of words,
no soft rumble rises as thunder over a solemn lake.

Instead, a swan glides making a no-sound.
Words collide, smudge together.

This is how I hear words: slight corrections.
It reminds me of when people think they hear something,

but what was said had an entirely different meaning,
which we cannot hear over our arguments.

How My Six-Year-Old Son Learned Counting

I started with toy cars.
He realized some were red,
some had four doors,
some were racers, some were trucks. He asked,
how do I count them?

I used Cheerios.
I made sure they were exact sized.
We counted and un-counted them.
I added; he ate and subtracted.

This was what it came down to:
his memorizing by rote, a myna bird,
blasted out numbers into one word:
onetwothreefourfivesixseveneightnineten.

He was thinking:
these cars are different, these O's are different,
but how do I group them?

I used rows of cars for multiplication;
he devoured a row of Cheerios for division.
By noon, we moved to Particle Physics.
We decided that holes in Cheerios represent Black Holes.
The cars were no longer random elements.
We considered singularities and existence winking out.

His kindergarten teacher complained:
Why does he talk about the Chaos Theory?
It upsets others
to know we will all become extinct someday.

Universal Sign for *Silence* is a Hush Finger to Lips

A soothing drizzle — sound of stillness,
what are you trying to tell me?

My deaf father was not born deaf.
He lost his hearing in a war
and/but refused to learn sign language.

Rain asks, why does silence have so many languages?

I loosely filter my fingers downward
as a sign for *rain*. *Rain* as a verb.
My father wanted words

filtered into long-faced vowels,
forced and explosive consonants.
He wanted me to shape words with my mouth.
Words as verbs.

To make the sign for *stubborn*, I cross my arms
and pout. Children know this one.
Father refused to learn it.
Instead, he held a dictionary of silence,

knowing stillness has a beating heart,
and just because he couldn't hear sound doesn't mean
noise isn't everywhere. Silence hurts.

I know sign language for *pain*.
I hit a fist into an open palm and make a face.

Words drizzle — soft intentions,
fingerspelling *loss*.
He can't hear how I struggle to be heard.

Signing for *love* mimics a heart traveling to another.

I Keep Anticipating a Phone Call

Rain whispers
what I know is true:
                    my son has left.

I know how emptiness feels —

                    a man pacing floors; a needy rain
sharp as pins and needles, fixed in time
and space; a son in detox.

Emptiness keeps calling,   staring through me.
          How incredibly miserable rain is.

It's difficult waiting.
                    I cradle silence.

          Some rain never seems to touch ground.

It's hard,   not absorbing what's happening.

          I know stillness.
                    It whispers.

My Father in a Noise-filled World

This world can be
a silent place —

noiseless birds
stirring hushed leaves;

words moving strangely,
tranquil elements of surprise.

Our world can have silent,
ruffled words

wind stirs.
Such a quiet, quiet world.

Such a speechless world,
a place where words on lips

unfold secrets,
one vowel petal after another.

Summertime and Living Was Not Easy

1.

There was space enough for turtles and frogs
collected in a box my mother would empty
back into a local pond. Summer
meant *exploration*, strange as fireflies
being snuffed out. Our nearest neighbor
lived a mile too close,
a mere horse canter.
We'd leave on a Coleman lantern,
and our light was mistaken for an oncoming train
or a fallen full moon limping in pain.

My piano music comforted those who needed solace
in this absolute distance. My music would carry far
with no interruptions. My piano notes
were mistaken, too — for pond water
when a loon slid across.

2.

Summer lasted long enough, folding
wings when resting.
I'd never try to disturb those days. Rain
fell emphatic, banging its kettle drum.

Try wrapping your arms around sunlight
to save for winter; it can't be done. I tried.

I saw a yellow spotted frog
extend its elongated arms and legs,
trying to reach both sides of a pond,

then, I got an idea of gathering light.

3.

When trains clattered, deer would run the ridge.
When a red caboose passed by,
the sun would lower, a striated rock,

plop into our pond.

I would hear far-off neighbor's porchlights sigh.

4.

Sky was kneaded dough.
Cooling-off period ended.

I pulled a clothesline,
pulley moving rope,
sun still hanging on it,
a wet swimsuit held by two pins.

A loon sounded a wail and bark,
while a purple honeysuckle opened to hear
one of my music notes
as it splashed in the pond.
I made music with no intention.

A catfish with long strange whiskers
twitching like fireflies in a Mason jar
when someone forgot to put nail holes in a lid.

5.

Mother was snapping peas, rocking absentmindedly
while the sun continues its jazz riff
in spidery willow branches.
Peas, green and round, spilled out of shells
into a tin bucket where I had stored frogs.
Peas sounded a tuned piano
with a string broke.

A train drowsed by.
Father was searching for a job with less stress.
His mouth opening and closing as a honeysuckle
as he read aloud his possibilities.
Words jumped as frogs. A quilt snapped on a clothesline.
Wind picked up a notch.

Summer was unbinding its wounds.

Neighbors would argue, and we'd never hear it this far away.
Their disagreement smelled with oncoming rain.

Mother was too busy to gossip.

6.

A sonata note transformed into a moon,
a hummingbird's eye, a pond with no name.

As soon as the moon disappeared, sun appeared,
a child's magic trick everyone has seen before.

Clear sky reflects light shining dewdrops.

A train came to rest more than a stone's throw away,
a pause between musical intervals.
Whizzing insects slowed down as fall approached.
Tail end of a rainstorm's last drops would settle.

As I was practicing Brahms, notes hopping
frogs, mother's voice snapped as pea shells.

Once, we let lights go out,
a loon serenaded all night to coax it back.

I caught my mother emptying my box of frogs.

What They Never Tell You About Growing Up

In order to get somewhere in a canoe,
you must paddle one side, the other.
To coax a rowboat, you must
stroke both paddles together,
or you'll spin endlessly in a circle.

A kingfisher anticipates fish
in perfect stillness.

You stop paddling, halt talking, hold breath
as if it was a firefly in your hand,
while a boat coasts as silent as aging.

They never tell you this when you're growing up —
all these motions you must muddle
and paddle through. They never tell you
life or a boat can come to a standstill.

They definitely never tell you
fish you see swims somewhere else, or that fish
swims as a metaphor for all you are waiting to catch.

They certainly never tell you
we do not need anchors or reason or randomness
to choose where we want to be.

In order to see dawn, go before light
sneaks up — a mere whisper at a time,
making birds start their engines.
You can't see where night ends
and landfall begins.

Sometimes, sound moves as a water moccasin
slithering under.
Once in a while, you hear plops
and can't identify where they are.
Sometimes, water speaks.

The Mockingbird Mimics the Out-of-Tune Grand Pianos in the Extravagant Neighborhoods

Based on Bob Herz's translation of Jules LaForgue's "Songs of Pianos in Rich Neighborhoods"

1.

My parents could not afford a piano.
I saw one in a choir loft, sat down, without asking,
played what I had only heard on the radio,

Mozart's *Minuet and Trio in G Major* —

I was five, and could not reach the foot pedals
to dampen tone, did not know it was intended
for a harpsichord,

I had to play it, by ear,
memory from hearing it once.
I did not know
he wrote and played it when he was my age,

his first piece, ambitious,
annoyingly perfect composition
architecturally designed.

A priest ran out complaining,
how dare I commit such a sacrilege?
But my parents were convinced I needed a piano,
even if they had to save up for one over time.

2.

I love to play with windows open,
see if birds would join in.

By seven, I was in a local symphony orchestra.
We were so poor I had to memorize sheet music.
I learned to tie a bow tie,
finding the right notes, by practice.

I loved the audience, first laughing at my size,
then mesmerized,
until they were lost in my forest of hands.

3.

Classical composers needed patrons —
a count or a duchess with a child unable to focus,
to take months of patience
to unwrap their child's ability to locate one note,
maybe two. Time to work on their operas
or symphonies on the side.
Composers needed time, lodging, and money.

All I had for support was
whatever I was paid for raking leaves.

4.

One day, my hands began shaking,
sound dropping out of my hands
as stillbirth calves.
My hearing abandoned me. Sparrows stopped singing.
Streets grew quiet.

I could see children playing,
screeching intense joy. Silence entered my ears
and hands, but the memory of sound rested in my heart,
a whisper, an echo of past intention, a slumbering dirge
I could not play,

and I walked away,
a rejected lover.

5.

I walk as a snow flurry.
The sun, a dampened foot pedal,
controls the softness of the moment.

All gone now. Well-placed fingering.
Deaf as a piano. The crush of snow

under my boots no longer crunches.
Boredom of girl's dreams.
Blank verses. Odes to what-could-have-been.
Empty pianos translate answers.

I walk through a forest as if between sections of sheet music,
blackbirds hanging onto each note in scales.

When Beethoven could not hear,
he amputated the legs off his pianos,
close to the floor,
to the heartbeat of the earth,
vibrations, sound traveling over time,
distance to ear, brain,
impatient hands.

I did not do that. I could not maim my best friend.
It was painful to walk away.
Leave music abandoned on someone's porch step,
a baby with a note. A whole note,
big enough to walk through with Hopi
climbing into The Fourth World leaving the flood behind.
I could walk away,
hear Bach's *Brandenburg Concerto, number three,*
in G Major —

Phrygian half-cadences —

o, absence and presence, simple rages
of loss, abeyance of weather and mockingbirds,
affluent mansions I pass by and cannot enter.

I can handsaw legs off the world,
place my weak ears so close to the earth,
ears melting into the earth,
earthworms singing,
crushed sea shells under the earth
coiling and recoiling noise.

6.

Our world contains riffs

of other peoples' stories and voices —
odd, unplayable —

the juxtaposition of accidentally heard phrases
passed down, decompartmentalized,
homogenized into drinkable satisfaction,

refurbished
old cane chairs
with weak interwoven seats,

regurgitated, spewed, redirected,
a river, until the original music garbles
beyond recognition

by my temperamental ears.
My own useless, irresponsible ears.

I don't hear rain falling.

7.

To which I add my composition,
my decrescendo,

soft melody,

one that does not blend or intend to blend
sparrows in a field of hundreds of sparrows,

one, easily replicated by mockingbirds,
one estate matching another estate in rich,
untouchable neighborhoods,

where I never belonged, longed to belong,
out of reach —

I can no longer hear or play:
snow on a piano; lingering
goodbye kisses
by adorable people;

kisses opening matinee cards
explaining tonight's haunting rendition
of misery; unspeakable;
one hand collapsing music;

a forest of silence
filling with softening snow;

cooing doves
I pull out of the magic of my sleeves,
white as an absence.

I sit on a stool
in front of a piano
not there

play what I hear
in the vacuum,
when audiences disappear,
a magic trick, a trick of lights,
an illusion or an allusion,

imagery lit on candelabras.

O, silence,
o, silence of silence,
o, hushed movement of hands,

o, disembodied silence of hands,
keys on a grand piano.

8.

I write sheet music,
flickering sounds in my hands,

what I know,

what I don't know,
its dissonance.

9.

Birds listen to me composing this coda,

end of my serenade
flutters out of my window
black and white piano keys.

10.   Music in Minor Key

Now that I'm older, I play minor key on piano
of life, using no dissonant chords, no extra flourishes.

I've been to burnish fields. Jonquils
by miles. A squabble of geese passes,
absorbed in urging to leave before snowfall,
while longing stays strong
and currents tug invisible strings. Days are
brusque languages, too quick to hear, too close
to heart to ignore, their formal grace
leaving me behind.

I play this slower,

but I continue to speed read through life
all their disappointments, missed opportunities,
unerring fierceness and passion.

I do best with the little I have before an audience fades.
Time to be alone, a single stanza
not touched, sun not finding every flower,
every absorbent fern, every lyric in river water.

Turning sheet music to find
you hiding between lines, stanzas
and pauses. And there, a night watchman
watches over me, pacing darkness.
As gentle as first snow, composing
into another day; there I'll be, trying to play what I see —

no sharps, no flats,
just joy, unbounded, unrequited joy.

Sign Language with Watery Movement of Hands

I lift a bouquet of spring water from my hands
to my mouth — a brass band celebrates gratitude
in my heart. The sign for *love* is universal.

This sign for "*water*" is to flow a hand across your body.
To say "*memory*," touch your head with an index finger.
There's no sign for "*drinking well*." I must finger-spell

these words. I taste the deepness of earth, its music,
my thirst for answers, torrents forming
stories about the water in our bodies.

When I spend all day by an ocean,
splash-whoosh of waves sings me back to creation.
The sign for "*whoosh*" is clapping two hands.

I can reach into sea grass at ocean's edge,
feel small fish in their nurseries.
Wiggle a hand across your body to sign "*fish*."

Springs and rivers
merge into the energy of oceans.
The sign for this churning makes an explosion.

And my memory suddenly shifts to places long gone:
wrecked over time and human carelessness.
I don't like to sign "*drought*" or "*disaster*."

I know without water, we will die.
Right now, someone drinks contaminated water.
Lakes and rivers are drying up.

What signs can I give this world
to change future's course?
My hands can form words,

but they cannot make them
flow
into that delta of your ears.

Hiding Place, a Place of Riddles

I know cruelty includes children
whose faces scrunch-up in hatred.
No word *homesickness*
when neighborhoods terrorize me.
Only hiding place
becomes where I am invisible
when I close my eyes.
Happy becomes a boy whose fear
leavens into bread.

I know tiny flames of silence.
I was taught well: keep low,
close to heartbeat of ground.

A cathedral of shrubs in my backyard
promise *Sanctuary. The King of the Lost World*
becomes one who sees no reason to return.

One night, I sleep in my hiding place
and no one notices I am missing.
My body does not know how *relaxed* feels.

For a night, I forget my brother
threatened to whack me with a hammer
to see if I would crack open like a piggy bank.
He has already practiced on several frogs.

I debate wisdom of returning.

Hearing Indirectly My Son Needs Drug Rehab

Darkness places its palms on the ground.
I cannot prevent this intense surprise from entering me.

I must break down what I hear
into manageable, bite-size pieces.
I did not expect to be uprooted by this news —
it hurts to hear it.

My simple tools of questioning
turn on lights inside the house of my heart,
until I murmur with answers —
let him go, let him go, let him find his own solution.

And then darkness releases its grip on my world,
stops staring.

I toss out my concerns. Darkness
notices
a blue light emanating from my body.
And yes,
darkness trembles,
thrown back on its haunches,
unable to fight
my light, magnifying as I release guilt.

Phone Call

I receive a phone call: *your father is dying.*

I drop whatever I am doing. *Too late*
always makes worse news for memory to hear.

I'm too far away to make it in time,
across the country in Georgia.
If I want to say goodbye thank him,
I have to do it by phone,
but in the half-light a phone makes no sense.

He arrives at a hospital half-dead,
dies on his way to a room.

It's a nasty hot Georgia night,
deer move tentatively as I speed pass them.

On the phone, Mom says
he saw his death coming for months,
but he didn't want to concern me.

She wants me to know that I do not have to worry,
he eased into his death as if it was bedroom slippers.

Mom says they will hold up his funeral until I arrive.

I am four hours from nearest airport. I drive
through night and Georgia heat,
a directional arrow.

I do not understand
why no one tells me anything.

The Grief Counselor

It began with the first war wounded I brought back
as a medic, when he realized that he wasn't going to make it
because the surgeons moved on. He asked me
to write his wife and children about his death.
How do I put such words into action? I began
as if passing out scalpels. At first, words were sluggish
like the double-yoke water buffalos in Vietnam.
Each word arrived easier, as I eased into the explanation.
I do not recall what I wrote. My heart shattered into rice.
So many peace doves flew into my pen.
I looked at the family picture of his wife,
his ten-year old daughter, the letter informing him
that he would be discharged soon. The word "soon" hurt.
Explaining to a child was the hardest letter.

Sure, they would get a form letter from the government,
impersonal and impassionate. I couldn't allow
the dead to not be able to pass on a message.

I would see many more letters exactly the same,
more pictures of girlfriends, wives, parents.
The word "soon" always arrived too late.
So many blank letters to fill and send,
trying to make sense out of the senselessness of war.
Letters about the ones never coming back,
countless letters, sometimes reporting missing limbs,
about attaching prosthesis. Too many one-way letters,
but occasionally, someone would write back
thanking me for my kindness to their loved one.

After a while, I got better at addressing grief,
because often I was the one that carried them back.
I was the one helping with surgery, the one
zipping body bags, looking for name tags.

A lot of the return letters asked how to stop war,
its unstoppable nature. I suggested
contact a legislator, join a protest movement,
stuff I was not supposed to suggest.
I couldn't answer any other way.

Learning the Hard Way

Times when our cat brings in a limp blue jay,
plopping it, an offering; or,
when my son's friend dies without any reason;
or, when police fire into peaceful protestors
with rubber bullets and tear gas;
my son moves from childhood to adult at ten.

Saying, *its God's plan*, does not answer a child.
Answers do not overcome natural curiosity.
A child has a "*why*" for every answer.

How does a parent explain the complex, simply?
There are no easy answers, no shortcuts,
no simple reasons. Problems accelerate,
branch out. I try to get to the root of them.
I need a good shovel. All of life intermingles.

I dig deeper.
I can spend my whole life trying to answer,
but I never know all reasons myself.

My son wants answers:
Why can't my friend come to play anymore?
Why are people cruel to people? Why sadness?
Why do you plant seeds knowing they could fail?
Will I die someday? Why's death necessary?

I have no easy answers and still don't.
But I begin with the hard ones.

Everything is Connected

It's pointless to regret what might have been.
Just ask my father about the Second World War,
when his cannon backfired,
killing everyone else immediately, and leaving him deaf.
He knew what it was like to be covered in blood splatter.

I can picture my father, limp on red ground,
when some field medic, checking for pulses,
brings him back to safety. War explodes time.

I know the loneliness of choices,
as a field medic in Vietnam,
how survivors feel guilty making it alive,
other men never going home.

I can almost see my father
waking up on a cot in a hospital, unable to hear
some doctor asking, "Can you follow my finger?"
The doctor's lips moving silently,
my father not responding.

I also know this story:

my father had a war buddy
who promised to fix him up with a woman he knew.
She worked in a factory where they made weapons
that helped increase killing.
When she witnessed all those wounded men
next to my father, she quit her job.
She became my mother.

When I received my draft notice for Vietnam,
my mother hid the mail. She knew war subtracts,
leaves some wounds you never see.

I volunteered to be a medic. I couldn't imagine killing.

War numbs many of us. I know what it's like
to walk through fields of dying and wounded men,
needing to leave the dying behind.
I touched death. It felt human.

My mother never forgave me for being that close to death.

My father never told me what it was like to be a survivor;
I had to learn the hard way.

My mother tip-toed around problems, biting her tongue,
frustrated with his deafness.

I could never tell my son about war,
although he loved playing with toy soldiers.
He might have thought it odd when I suggested
needing a toy medic, although he never said anything.

We never know where life goes,
and choices narrow into vanishing points.
Not being able to talk out issues
leaves scabs on a heart.

And, I have to admit,
I could not tell him the toll war had taken on me.
I could not talk about Vietnam for years.
I kept those secrets inside me,
a locket of misery.

I still have problems talking about it.

War creates another type of deafness.
I am trying to remove those bandages of silence.

It's time to carry out the wounded.

Champions of the World

trickle-down pine-snow
had an attitude
nothing could stop it

this strange transition of last snow
impulsive water

stir-crazy
from cabin fever
loose-wild
my son
pent-up
all springy and wound-up
finally releasing

a clap of crows
spiked upwards into warmer air
away from bare elm branches

after this break long silence
purple crocuses
wake up
shouting

singing
*We are the champions
of the world*
as we scuffled
through snow

kicking loose flakes
into dust

time-period between disappearing snow
emerging life
rubbery and distorted
with unpredictability

crows flew away
protesting our off-key singing

How Death Works

I had a friend die on April First.
At first, I thought that phone call was a prank,
some cruel April Fool's joke. It wasn't.
We were young and stupid, and all of a sudden —
because that's how death works —
we weren't going to shoot basketballs anymore.

My father left behind his inheritance of loud ties
not even Goodwill wanted to accept.

My mother doubted her own existence,
until she didn't.

When my friend died,
I wanted to shoot the basketball backboard,
but didn't.

Death does not have a plan,
doesn't follow a regular work schedule.
It works
more like a nasty surprise.

I've known too many that died in Vietnam
from a bullet with a name on it.
I wrote letters to families for guys
missing hands or had died.

I'm getting better at eulogies.
Practice makes perfect.

To make the sign for *dead*
use a flat hand and move from one shoulder
to the opposite hip
as if rolling over.

II.

Traveling through Life with My Son

He persists as soon as we start,
how long before we arrive?
After a mile, a road extends to
are we there yet? We haul forever:

one ghost-shell of a nameless town
after another,
just boarded-up
has-beens, never-were places
with graffiti water towers,
unkempt fields gone seedy.

He's determined to find an end-it-all rest,
as I transfer from job to failure to unrest,
no sooner unpacking, then uprooting, again.
We never fully arrive, we never fully depart,
pulling up stakes, hammering them in,
yanking them out again.

He barely makes friends, learns their names,
leans into secret handshakes, and we're off
again, jiggety-jig. He can only glance back
at this unsteady world of what-might-have-been,
as if we're easily transplanted tomatoes.

What happened to that child
who wanted to get some place fast?

What happened to me,
never finding roots
in the many places we stayed?

Somehow, somewhere, he went a different way,
never arriving where he wanted to be.
He's determined to be restless,
not getting anywhere.

I keep opening road maps
trying to find him.

Listening to a Meadowlark

A meadowlark called over empty fields
of broken clay. I want to be that song,
that flight, to find an overview
past frustration that comes
with planting and being a part of nature.

During intervals between songs,
I will break earth
or earth will break me,
while that meadowlark
travels over distances I can't even see.

A lark left its song behind as a feather.

This world will either be a hard place
where I uproot fieldstones bigger than my plow,
or a fertile one, depending on unreliable weather.

Rains may bless us or we might be cursed
by extreme heat, but still a song
finds its way to people willing to listen,
pulls a person out of grief
to a different place.

Perhaps this is what my grandfather meant,
when he would say, "It's in God's hands."

But am I not in God's hands
as I push a hand plow,
breaking ground and physics of resistance?

I hear a song, ground giving way,
music fading in the sky with a lark.

Memorial Tree

My mother answers me, saying
my father lost his hearing during war.
I cannonball outside to search for it.

In a childish fit, I bury some toy German soldiers,
plant a memorial tree, scream bloody murder
into the cider-dark night.
I am told to keep it down; people are sleeping.

Years later, I find a pirate map I drew
showing those toys' location.
The green plastic won't decompose,

even though someone pruned that memorial tree
into nothingness,
empty branches raising in surrender.

Sometimes, childhood makes no sense;

we prune back memories
until empty branches remain.

Summer of My Seventh Year

Hundreds of millers hover
and smash against our porch light.
Those moths lodge and struggle to get free
off mesh screen door,
white wings beating frantically.
Night's perfect for last acts.

Soon, we'll slog to school again,
answering teacher's question,
what did you do all summer?

I'll say, *Nothing.*

How can I say I was able to pack
a lot of stupidity in three months,
kill my share of minutes, spinning
in circles, as dizzy as millers, slam
our screen door going in and out
of chores, mostly avoiding them,
until they stack up. I get into more trouble
than I can avoid. If you ask me, I won't say I am
stir-crazy, ready to burst out of my skin.
That if I can swarm into a bright light
I probably would, just to know how it feels.

I don't know what drives me,
or any man, but I do my best to go through the motions
playing *war* all day, shooting cap guns.
No one wants to come in,
although our mothers roll-call.
Why's war so fascinating?

My dad never talks about it. I wish he would.
I know there's something
I need to know.

In the Storm

My son phones, and my heart narrows into joy.
My son doesn't call often. I suspect he needs money.
My dreams cast out thousands of possibilities.

My son tells me he doesn't want to see me again.
No reason given. Just a quick message, then gone.
He flies out of my heart.

It starts raining, accumulating recklessly, a flash flood.
Noah sent a raven out from the Ark, and it never returned.

A robin pecks on my window, delivers a spiritual message.
Sparrows fly off as soon as I leave to see my son.
My mind searches for meaning where there is none.

It's so nasty wet and cold outside.
I scoop up a bird's lifeless body,
trying to decide what to do with it, what to do
with my loss, what this world warns me of
when I am not listening.

Hot Chocolate

To me, hot chocolate will always be after trudging in snow,
dragging my sled, its metal blades cutting two lines.
I'd climb what I thought was a dangerous hill
because it ended at ongoing traffic. After several slides,
I'd triumphantly returned more ice than snow.
I'd seemed forever to exit the snowsuit mother
zipped me into, all the way to my neck. My clothes soaked,
nose running, snowflakes still on my lashes.
After changing into dry clothes, I'd rush to the kitchen table,
to find a can with Ovaltine, pry it open, spoon out
the powder into a cup with hot water. I'd plop in
marshmallows, trying to make them ka-splash.
Those marshmallows swirled on top as white icebergs,
or clouds, or top hats. I'd try to dunk them, soften them up,
make them gooey. But they'd plop back up, unsinkable.
If I waited long enough, the heat would soften them
like first snowflakes. I'd regale my daring deeds
of sledging to my horrified mother,
who feared identifying my body under a speeding car,
gripping the rope that guided the sled. I never knew
she faked it, trying to strike fear into me
and my self-preservation.

It was a simple life then, where life melted and blended,
the darkness of winter like chocolate, the hot furnace
filled of coals that had rumble down the coal chute.
I've gone back as an adult, found the sled
with its metal runners, stacked where the coal furnace
used to be. All gone. My mother dead.
The hill not as steep as I remembered,
the traffic not as fierce and flowing. I had to return,
had to glance one last time at my childhood,
realize I could not return. This fact was driven into me
when I could not find Ovaltine or a bag of marshmallows.

And, it seems to snow less now. The days of packing
snow forts and tossing snowballs seem over.
Every moment has stirred too fast, blended too fast.
I am no longer the daredevil, speeding on a sled,
unzipping a snowsuit of mostly snow.
Most of all, my mother cannot hear my tales of terror
while I waited for the hot chocolate and marshmallows to blend.

I Knew You When You Were the Beginning of a Sentence

I knew you
as quiet listening,
a grey heron becoming the only cloud in sky
after enduring a long day.

I can't count stars any more —

it's impossible to do
when your absence enters my heart,
an end of a song.

Your voice used to undulate
blackbirds
making calligraphy across the sky.

Days churn endlessly for me,
as I turn pages of life to see what follows next.

I want you to return,
even if you appear as just a yellow warbler
returning to a branch
in hush-breeze.

A green, green leaf
flutters in sky:

a heart in grief.

The sky makes sign language for *sorry*,
a "y" shape hand
with a thumb of raindrop
twisting on my chin.

When Water Creates Sound

I recall a movie I saw in fifth grade
about Helen Keller as a deaf-blind child.

Her teacher pumped water onto Helen's hand,
teaching Helen to sputter words,
a rush of sounds, water mixing.

Helen struggled,
stammering near-sounds,
recognition flooding her face
with her eureka moment: *Water*!

How simple Helen's teacher made it all seem.
To make the sign for *water*,
separate the three middle fingers
while holding the thumb and pinkie finger together.
Then tap your index finger on your chin a couple of times.

But there must have been trial and error,
while I tried ways to make my father hear.
There must have been frustration, shrugged defeat;

When I tried ways to make my deaf father hear me.
his face was often as blank as blackboard slate.

Unlike that teacher, I failed
in communicating sounds of objects
my father once heard. I only kept
repeating myself, unheard.
Silence became his comfortable chair to sit in,
one where he could kick back, relax.

Sometimes, he'd catch a word
as if it were a bird loose in our house.

Sometimes,
words might as well had been water
slipping through his fingers.

Son, My Chronology Ends with You

Believe me, son,
you will come to a house
at a certain age, and you will not own that key.
Your empty arms will be testaments to what you do not have,
and your life will become inertia.

So, I made you this origami boat.
It can be as big as your imagination,
or as small as promises you never kept.

Receive this boat, wide as your arms,
launch it forward; it's yours.

Now, I set you out on it,
straight into perpendicular sunset.
Canvas jib sheet tries to catch wind
as if it was a comet tail.

Make the turn,
shifting rudders. Then,

you are gone.

You are gone
over into vanishing horizons,
lavender skies ahead,
sun folding behind this landscape.

Shelling

One of us must speak, break conversation, repair it.

My father and I sit together without
talking, snapping open pea shells, six to a pod,

plinking into a bucket, a gentle-rain sound.

Some shells we eat, but not these: they're different.
We can't fix broken.

I toss the shells away like bullet castings
and roll our silence between my fingers.

I carry distance between us like a wounded soldier —
there are rules we break
and rules we keep,
solemn cross-my-heart-and-hope-to-die promises.

I need to talk about constant shelling during Vietnam,
but my tongue rolls,
plinks
into this bucket.
Metallic notes from an African thumb piano.

Each pea becomes a miniature world in a galaxy of music
pauses between us, worlds rolling between God's fingers.

Snap peas, *plink*, *plink*, *tink* — repetition numbs us
toward napping on this warm day, belly-full,
as the sun *plink*-snaps open clouds.

One of us must speak, break conversation, repair it.

But we don't,
stillness *plinking*. Bullets
never make round holes.

Our silence speaks volumes.

Manifestation

My mother keeps me in her head,
refusing to let me go
where goldfinches are active at my feeder.
So, I listen, a wailing wall, as she wails
from deep well of sadness.

As a child stirring mud
freshened by a sprinkler can of water
trying to find that right consistency,
I wanted to create a mud pie for dessert.
In background, birds were doing rounds
they taught at school,
how and when to enter after one group finishes
with layered waves of music. Even now,

in present time, I can see goldfinches
taking turns at my feeder, row
after yellow row. I wait to speak
when my mother's sobs subside and crash
against shores of this room.

I recall pride offering my mud pie,
leaving muddy palm prints on a doorknob,
tracks of brown footprints on our carpet.
My mother looked down, a curious god,
so that her glasses slid to her nose tip,
and declared it was too perfect to eat.

My mother bawls louder, a nose-honking sob,
declared she didn't want that story
or to remember yellow birds dancing at a feeder
and how she had to purge my clothes, plunging me
fully dressed in our claw bathtub, and waiting
for water to stop being coffee colored.

I thought the story might make her smile a crack,
but I made sadness worse.

A door to my mother's grief
locks me in shadows. I feel as useless as dad's shirts
empty and drooping in closet.

Even a deer, far away, in woods
beyond train tracks, holds its breath
afraid to exhale, not move so jerkily, not to stir
silence.

Silence is an empty birdfeeder, the way it sways
when birds realize there isn't any more.

I sit and listen to sadness gather steam,
a train barreling down tracks. I sit
in my mother's grief,
do the only thing I can do:

I listen.

Occupation of Hands

Notice hands
moving since morning,

releasing sparrows
into cracks of light
through stared-at fingers.

Once released, sparrows divide
into more sparrows,
until they sub-divide
into houses
the size of small hands.
Each fingernail, a window,
darkens with rain.

Notice your hands
until they become glass.
They are always turning a page
of an instructional manual
to see what to do next.

Sometimes, instructions are braille.
Sometimes, they speak another language.
Sometime, words crumble when touched.
My hands finger spelling or using sign language
and my deaf father refusing to learn sign.

Look at all the loss a hand can/cannot hold.

Story of Absence

In watercolors, leave blank spaces
for a viewer to fill in.

An empty net needs filling, says a fisherman,
to silent reflective lake.

Grandma says, *leave one imperfect stitch,
and an eye will balance it.*

My father tangled in deaf-silence,
piecing together meaning,

the importance that absence hints at
in improvisational jazz.

In watercolors, it is helpful to move fast,
let colors collide, let dry, hope impression lasts.

My mother says
my *imagination seems bedeviling,*

A hummingbird left behind
its impression

of here-and-gone, an emptiness
filling what sometimes should be left blank.

Talking to My Brother

We sit below wheeling starlings,
punctuating quiet with their etchings.

Perhaps, I should start.

It's been so long since we've really talked.
I could say, *the weather
remains unpredictable.*

As long as rain holds,
we talk,

rekindling this way,

one step forward,
two more awkward steps,
three easier.

I have some bridges to mend
now that my brother has cancer.

It took a major disease to bring us together
after years of being afraid of him
as a child when he chased me with a hammer.

At least we are talking.

It takes courage to hug him,
feel his fear of dying,
a storm approaching.

We do not hold back.

Words begin,
like a murmuring of starlings
skywriting *grief*.

Now we are speechless.
No words need to be said.

The rain doesn't dampen this day.

A River Rushing By

A dream-fish flounders in my arms,
light glints off its scales
I throw it back into the memory-lake,
but its weight still lies solidly in my arms.

My son doesn't want to admit we are connected.
In fact, he wants to obliterate that fact.

I could tell him about our similarities,
but he doesn't want to hear my voice.

He doesn't want to know what he needs to know.

In my dream, trees dangle their leaves,
reminiscent of bait on fishing lines,
a mere loon's cry from another shore.

When my son was born, he was a part of me.
An invisible river connected us and divided us.
Now, he's that river rushing by
trying to get somewhere else.

The more he denies, more it remains true.

When I tossed that dream-fish,
it arched silver and yellow,
a directional arrow towards home.

That fish and loon were never here.
My son swims on his own.

Letter to My Son

When you outgrew my stories,
you did not care
if I sang you to sleep, or watched over
dreams on your face.

Ten times a night I would pace
and perch
at every breath.
How I miss those opportunities.

Traveling difficult paths
of child moving towards adult
convinced there was no map
in the book.

You wouldn't have believed me
if I told you there was.

Still, you were never a burden. I carry that weight
of your infancy on my arm, a tattoo.
When I held you,
all stories and songs began.

Now, I forget stories, songs lose their melodies.

At this distance, tell me,
are you alright?
My dreams of you
jump as terrified sheep.

Message Was Delivered

I know where I am going, he insisted,
and I know I don't belong there.
My father was measuring
doubt
while asking forgiveness.

I'll send you a message
to let you know I made it,
he promised, adding, *I was not so bad;*
I'd seen worse, done worse.

Then, he was gone — a breath pushed out,
I hoped he heard me wishing him well.
I never really expected a message;
not even in a bird's octaves.

But I swear the roof opened up that day,
his soul venturing tentatively out,
bounding from his body.

My brooding
lifted and the
margins of love
swung open.

I knew he was accepted,

flaws and everything,
soul polished, almost blinding me.

You'd have to witness
such a transformation to believe it.

But I'll tell you this: I never expected to see him
inside that incredible light,
even after I did.

Even after I had
second-thoughts,
I had to nail down the roof
with the same difficulty of trying to explain to others
without sounding like I was insane.

Sonata

Sun-rich, in a translucent stream, breeze-free,
thrum-sound spills to a larger river,
passing white pines, a solemn prayer.

My near-deaf father died quietly:
a dragonfly over glass-water;
lark-song in a red garden of intention.

My prayer flew indirectly,
a paper kite butterfly.

Dawn swept in.
Loss lodged:
a peach pit in my throat.

Mourning has terraces,
revelations of love and grief,
lightning striking,
brief, quiet, after-calm.

Sometimes, a soul returns with its music,
nests inside a heart
a constant stream of memory.

My father taps on my window
when I hear ticking rain.

And when my mother died quietly,
a murmuring of starlings,
her soul everlasting waters,
I was convinced —

love never ends;
it's always beginning and reaffirming.

I Call This "Dipping Hands in Water to Feel How this World Moves"

I'm sure there's more to life than curiosity.
The yellow line of morning changes
architecture of each day
into a bridge of sighs.

Rejoicing birds
confirm there will be always more if I look
with certainty.

The world turns watery and elusive when touched —
what remains can be empty.

I want to hold objects,
feel their braille
like dirt
after a dry spell fragments.

I call this "*touch starved.*"
I call this "*building the bulk of senses.*"
I call this "*a bridge where we can meet
in a middle to talk in a common language.*"

Meanwhile, my hands busy themselves,
touching that elusive
blue aura around a person's head.

I Had Been Expecting This Phone Call Since January

I hoped I was wrong.
Unfortunately, his voice on the other end
confirmed what I knew had to be true.

"Mom died in her sleep."

I felt sorry for my son
passing on this information.

At least she died in her sleep,
someone would say, eventually. This
kind of news I expected.

Some would say
it was a relief she died;
painless, in her sleep.

People always say this
when they do not know what else to say.

I do not know what to say to my son
to ease his pain,
when often I lack the necessary words.
Some experiences in life
are not explained easily.

Life's hardest lessons
leave no rational justifications.

We muddle through trauma
hoping sadness eventually fades away.
And it's hard work;
often memory-pain returns at the worst moments.

Yes, she died in her sleep.
It was expected, and then
it happened quietly.

Unfortunately, my son witnessed her death.
It will hover in his heart for a long time.

I cannot tell him how long his sadness will last,
or how sadness ebbs and flows,
boomerangs back,
because each person enters grief differently,
and grief has no set time limit
how long suffering will last.

There's no manual to explain how grief works.
Loss is experiential.

I held onto the silence in the telephone call
like a lifeline to my son.
I knew he was drowning
and there are no words
to soothe his kind of pain.

Silence lasted for a long time.

III.

Everything She Ever Knew She Never Knew Again

(My mother was dissolving at the hospital.) She walked through a
wall into a startling forest of snow: "oh,   my,   goodness,
 I do so much love snow." And she felt no chill in her red flannel
pajamas.
Her dead brother skated up to her like Hans Brinker,
bragging,   *look at what I can do.*
She wanted to warn him about that thin ice he would break
through in a matter of minutes, but her words froze in mid-air.
She took a handy icepick and chipped away so that he can hear
her warnings, but her words
fell onto ground,
and at that moment, he crashed through crackled ice,
into a wormhole.

She tried to pick up her words
that squirmed away, wriggling. But trees carried her over
landscapes to where Summer was inside a log cabin, smoking a
corn cob pipe. Summer wouldn't let her in no matter how much
she knocked and pleaded. She wanted to sit by fire and reminisce
about by-gone days flying past her
                              ripped pages from a daily calendar
galloping into a horizon no longer there.

And our world was fragmenting faster than she could rubber
cement it together.

She worked with all the King's horses and all the King's frantic
men wearing metal gauntlets making their work near-impossible.
(The hospital couldn't find her when she danced this fast.)
She stretched into a giraffe and hid among tallest, leaf-driven
trees. She skated over sky, poking her head through clouds.
                (The doctors were frozen in place.)

She skimmed over those glossy parts of this world,
a speed reader.   Her blood thinned into mercury.
No one told her it would be this way:

she could glide over loss.   No one told her
how loss is tangible/intangible. No walls could tell her. No fire
escape. No secrets about recovery from loss.

Symphony of Quiet

When I lost partial hearing from shelling
in Vietnam, I finally understood my father.

If he was alive, I'd enunciate, "Dad, sparrow
songs are fading, the drip from faucets only
make sound when seen, shadows creep up
unexpectedly, toast no longer springs,
slippery roads don't slush, world tunes off
or dims sound."

A Great Length

Unmentionable silence keeps expanding.
My grief turns off a lit porch light
in darkness.

I talk to you although
you are not here.
I tell trees
and close curtains

in case you hear.

I keep losing hope.
I reach for a light switch.
I cannot believe what keeps you away can be so bad;
then I recall, hourly, daily,

you are not coming back.

Why a Little Bit of Elegant Fred Astaire Still Dances in His Heart

My father returns from the haberdashery,
strutting his sex appeal for my mother.
My father points to his new top hat covering his bald spot.
He asks, "Notice anything different?"

She unties her apron of tears. She needs money
for groceries.

But father is too busy being a peacock,
insisting a man's importance increases significantly
when wearing a dignified hat.

She nears boiling point.
I duck for cover. A rolling pin waits within reach.
But father waltzes around that argument. He cha-chas her.

My mother opens a Sears Catalog of complaints.
Father switches on the nightly news to watch
Kennedy's inauguration. Kennedy and Eisenhower ride
in a coach, wearing the same silk top hats
as my impressionable father.

It's an uncomfortably hot January in Washington, DC.
Kennedy removes his hat.
Every president after Lincoln had worn top hats.
Even men losing their shirts during the twenties stock market crash,
leapt from tall buildings, wore top hats. Even a common man,
like my father, saved pinched pennies, to purchase a top hat.

My mother swoons. Kennedy replaces Elvis as her heartthrob.
My mother points, "Now *that's* a good-looking man,"
with heavy emphasis on the word *that*.

At that precise moment, hats took a nose dive,
a whole culture shift earthquaking under my father's feet.

Calculus of Love

Had my father married someone other than my mother,
I'd have been someone else. Luck has timing
and percentages. Love has elemental properties —
wind, air, earth, blind luck, accidental occurrences.
Too often, love gives sparingly:
tilling fields does not equal more crops.
I've been adding up all possibilities,
randomness of being me,

part alchemy, part end-result.
Our world turns lush with inspired happenstances.
I cannot calculate odds that add up to me.
And now, I add you to this equation,
this intersection of us, this Venn diagram of us,
this lucky roll of dice of us.

Suddenness Flies in Swiftly and Exits Extremely Slowly
With two lines from Machado

Beat, heart… although mine stalled and fluttered,
a crane I once saw with a wounded wing.

     "How close was I?"

A doctor spread his thumb
and pointer finger: inches. I questioned mortality.
What caused this breach, showed my inevitability?

     Earth has not swallowed everything,
although my son said he never wanted to see me again.

My bad news was unexpected, just like that crane
when someone snapped its white wing
with an unsatisfactory snap. Both were unexplained,
leaving, instead, a void.

     What caused these shifts?

My heart broke.
     In an ambulance I pled, *Beat, heart…*

The doctor said I had a false heart attack.
It was more a false start, a stutter-step.
     Earth has not swallowed everything.

I saw someone take that crane to a vet.

Sometimes, wounds heal over time.
My pain remains unresolved, heart beaten,
stuck in this painful language of silence
with my bent-out-of-shape life, a broken wing.

I keep waiting for the unexpected to change.

It has been years since I've heard from my son.
I keep replaying same grief over
and over. Bitter music never changes,
never flies away.

After a vet repaired that crane's wing,
I saw that tentative crane released into air,

Sometimes, wounds heal over time.
No one ever knows how long healing will take.
I know recovery can be possible.
I've seen it happen.

> *Beat, heart…*
> *earth has not swallowed everything.*

Unfinished

My father tinkered on projects,
promising to finish them *someday*,
quickly accumulating another passion.

Today, clouds were incomplete.
I'd been to his grave a second time
to bury my mother's ashes with his.

I inherited a box of dad's unfinished plans.
They're buried in my attic
where I never seem to get to them.

Today, rain fell as heavy as hammers.
My brother sighed the same as our dad used to sigh
when unloading parts needing some assembly.

We went our separate ways,
left behind words
we'd say another day.

My Mother's *Forever House*

On my first birthday, my mother carried me
over the threshold to her *Forever House.*
It was raging snow in January.

She bundled me up,
covering my face from frost-bite danger
lurking in every hulking wind-blast snow-assault.

She told my father, "*Don't track snow in the house.*"
My mother proclaimed, "*I want to live here until I die.*"
It was royal decree mixed with prayer.

She pointed exactly where all her furniture would be,
making sure the beds were first to grace the house.
"*This goes here,*" she pointed, "*not an inch off.*"

My mother received her wish,
when they carried her out on a stretcher,
unable to command what to do next.

Emptying Time

While I was asleep, my father died,
slipped into that great coda, when memory passes
from one person to another person,
and I became a gatekeeper of his life.

And since there were gaps in his history,
I began filling them.

On my way to my father's funeral,
a large whooping crane wafts across the bay
where a lavender light floats on water.

Before the dead releases,
breath becomes one door closing,

another one opening.
That strange lyric
of a life that continues
when someone starts sharing a memory.

I wasn't there when he died,
but I have witnessed others at their last sigh
as a field medic in Vietnam. I remember
each of them like a slick country road
I must maneuver/drive in the dark.

The crane lifts its impossible weight,
its head matching crimson morning-break,
its *whoop-whoop* trumpets my loss.

How heavy a crane looks, large wingspan
almost tipping both edges of the sky,

endlessly suspended in air,
an aimless cloud, always present,
untouchable as thought.

Lastness of Silence

This world does not know true meaning of silence:
it disturbs, tears hearts. My son, my son,
where are you in this orange-red world? You left

      unsettling news. What could I do differently
      to change this terrible mockingbird song?

How could I have placed my thumb on these scales?
I find a distance between snapped hearts and no maps.
I walk as silent as this night, searching, searching,

      and you are not there. My son, my lost son,

lost within his own explanations. Answers are not here,
or in blank places in this sad jazz. My world empties.

You have not spoken to me since, my son, my son
of awful distances. This world cannot explain
true meaning of this silence, its haunting melody.

Gifts My Father Gave Me

1.

When my father died, quietly,
I started packing away his clothes.

Erasing him.

I went through a ritual for the dead;
pick up, clean up, tidy up their messes.

I found my father's hearing aid,
unused, unopened battery.

That sneaky, son-of-a-gun.

I never told my mother.

2.

I grew up shouting at my father,
who read my lips, saw my tongue placement,
watched my exaggerated
expressions of certain vowels,
explosion of consonants. I learned
silence and *noise* from him.

My father never could recall that connection
of sound to object,
before a war wound made sound watery,
silence closing off his ears.

My father struggled to hear,
straining his better ear towards the direction
he thought sound arrived.
Even then, he heard absolutely nothing.
Not even my mother's sweet nothings.

He needed tangible words he could feel with his fingers.

I'd get red in my face, screaming to be heard.
Often, he'd blink, noticing my mouth
moving like goldfish in a glass tank.

One time he tried hearing aids,
he complained about static feedback,
that kind I heard adjusting a radio knob
as I searched for a station while in the car.

He tried being sneaky, turning off his hearing aid
whenever my mother berated him.
She'd yell, balling her fists into ear plugs.

Years later, I still hear faint rumbling arguments,
lightning strike of hard words,
slow quiet when a storm gives in.

3.

My father taught me about wide silences between conversation
and not speaking, gaps when hemming and hawing
try to formulate proper words to say.

He discovered sounds of white noise,
electric feedback from touching a microphone,
or decibels of pitch broken and scattering.

Oh, how I wish he had tried harder to listen.
I tried sign language, but he wasn't interested.
He never seemed to want to hear what I said.

Loss of Hearing Makes an Ocean Wave Flat

A world without sound
still has noise. Ask the deaf —

there's static
from endless fields of faces.

Ask my father's conch shell ears
trying to remember any sound.

You might as well as ask many birds
why they do not sing.

Ask my hands translating for the deaf —
some words do not have sign language;

some words I have to fingerspell.
My hands have been talking for years.

My father hated sign language,
preferring people shout at him to lip-read words.

Ask my father why
he declined to learn; he won't hear you.

My father did not lose sound.
Sound lost him.

Escaping the Labyrinth

In a dark labyrinth, my mother insists
she's going for a walk with dad.
He's been dead ten years, come this January.
She does not have a ball
of string to unravel
and she's already lost.

Bed-ridden, a feeding tube
jammed down
her throat, gurgling,
a spring well
going dry,
another tube forced in her nose
to startle her lungs into functioning,
she's not
going anywhere soon. A nurse says,
it's to provide comfort, but it doesn't.
I want to let her ease into transition.

Instead, a nurse
flips her over.
My mother thrashes, a turtle kicking legs.
She remembers who we are,
then forgets,
a variation of Catch-Up.

She's back in 1940's.
She hadn't met dad, yet.
She's lucid, remembering.
Flash-points,
in and out. She falls desperately in love.

She wants out of here. She rants. She can't get up,
let alone walk, fused by wires and tubes.

I escort her wheelchair down maze-corridors.
She thinks her wheelchair is a carriage in snow.
Faster, she exclaims,
now we're getting somewhere.

Deafness in the Silent Language

An allegro of birds quickly passes by,
immaculate sheets of desperation and desire
through ribbons of sunlight. I can't hear them,

only their song trailing behind them,
like footsteps we hear too late. I can't explain this.
Instead, I fingerspell *expanse.*

Silent language includes brokenness.
Even gladioli become spellbound.
My world diminishes into a succession of hands,

quick paths to understanding
when someone cannot hear what is happening,
finds their ears, finding them closed.

I wave hands,
spell with fingers. How do I explain a sound
with no words: a soft timpani rain;

songbirds' many different tones; a horse hoof clap?
My fingers know apprehension and doubt trying
to explain sounds.

Interpretation of spoken language becomes approximation.
The departure of birds in *A sharp*
has a sound I cannot explain.

My fingers try to spell out the impossible and fail,
while a deaf person quizzically tries to understand.
Silent language always tries searching for understanding.

Playing Games with My Son

I still see myself crawling on floors
building wooden forts that I had cut and sanded
into squares, rectangles and triangles,
no rough edges.

We'd stack pieces
together, shoulder to shoulder,
architects.

I still have the blocks in my attic, collecting dust.

I'd get out of breath pushing him on swings
as he kicked
the sky. I talked more than I should,
taking oxygen out of every room.

Life has games with rules I do not understand.
Why can't I tell a story with a better ending?
It would be a lie to my heart otherwise.

I can't cut truth into shapes,
can't smooth edges.
Everything I built fell apart.
There are pieces of me in the attic, gathering dust.

My heart breaks into elegies for what-used-to-be
before sudden sharp turn, blocked arteries,
gasps, gaps between us.

    Drugs did that.

Elegy

The river darkens with amnesia: ten years ago, my father died.
But this memory also includes a gardenia,
their silk petals too weak for any storm or time.
Death becomes easy, bringing quickness, a promise.
Just in case, I took a picture of the flower
as it raptured into death. When my father died,
a loon began its swooning song,
scanning across silence, begging for love.
In spite of my father or the gardenia dying,
the sun and moon kept returning,
not caring about death or loss. I began wandering
a transient river, wanting to forget
and move on. I wanted to wash away memory,
make it drop like petals
in stop-motion photography. What I wanted
did not matter to the world spinning its calendar
trying to leave me behind holding grief
and its never-ending serenade. This is not about grief
or loss or regret. Those are about wrestling with death.
No. This is not about the undertow of memory flow,
how it keeps being agitated as it moves.
I want to disassemble sadness.
I want my song of endless searching,
a loon's quest,
to find love waiting for me.

The Shirt

I wait for rain to pass before taking laundry out.
Rusty creak pullies
move a line of clothes further when wet,
nearer when dry. My father is waiting.
Laundry will smell of lilacs
and front doors opening.

I lay out my father's shirt,
fold its arms over front,
hugging the shape of emptiness. I fold again,
neck to belly buttonhole.
I even button his shirt before folding.
I pack neatly.
My father is waiting.

I shake loose the laundry before folding,
stacking them in a wicker basket.
I snap sheets into distant thunder.

I lay out my father's shirt and iron.
His breast pocket will hold
his off-white monogram handkerchief.
I fold edges of his handkerchief
into silence.

I take his shirt as an offering to the undertaker.
Father would prefer this
pale blue.

Fishing with My Son

I purchased a tackle box, lures with silver hooks,
reel with line, and a box of
nightcrawlers, as big as my fingers.

Our lines whooshed-zipped like dragonflies
in perfect rainbow arches.
Hooks sank noiselessly,
bobbins plopped up.

We waited for fish that never bit,
while mosquitoes *zzzzed* near our ears.

It was a day I always wanted with my son:
alone,
shouldering nearer,
waiting for tug
of fish or sentences of acceptance.

Nothing said or heard,
brief soft noises,
one tentative verb at a time.

Silence held us close.

All that mattered was
one day with my son,
not needing to say anything,
when every unspoken moment spoke for itself,
no need to explain,

not knowing it would be our last time together,
he would cast me away,
turn to drugs.

And now I row my silent boat,
fishing for yesterday.

A Horizon is Vague at a Distance

I had tried to construct her memory,
but the image is grey winter clouds
before a snow storm breaks silence
in half, flakes like skin, yank-rips off
like bandages. I can't remember
the good days cross-stitched. Every
haunting footstep, every turnstile
to an exit or entrance, every spinning-
jenny making fragments, splintering
again, again. Memory is muddy now.
It's been too long, too many seasons,
too many things we never said, too
much shattering. When does memory
begin or end? splinters glass? I try
assembling pieces that don't fit.
I mold my mother's face out of clay.
Each particle of memory dissolves
as snowflakes on a tongue, crumbles
whatever we needed desperately to say.

The Day is Speechlessly Broken

Language of silence
slips secrets into brink
of other places.

My deaf father scuffling
on a deer trail, winding
through white pines
into shockingly
beautiful birds,
manifesting trees,
music's long flight
he will never hear.

I sign *songbirds*,

sign *this*
is music.

In My Near-Deaf Father's Dreams

he could hear people clacking like adding machines,
a long roll of numbers never adding up
to any good intentions.
Sound was whiteout when snow obliterates a road,
or chattering of locusts after their twelve-year emergence.

He kept searching for one sound
among a blizzard of silence. One noise shattering
limited possibilities. He did the best he could
with a broken lifeline with a hearing aid
failing him miserably.

If he heard God's voice, would it be a bluejay,
or a column of Roman numerals, or first snow
and the way it's always soundless and soulless?

Dreams tell us truth or fears, but we never listen
or forget them, or they linger
the way a bluejay lands and folds its wings,
or they vanish into a crowd of unrelenting voices.

I speak for the hearing impaired,
ears containing lack of music and pitch,
my hands conducting sign language
spelling, I hear you.

I want to say any number of words
about my father missing us saying his name
drifting as loose language of snow.
But I can't finger spell all this misery
as I too, lose my hearing.

I can't say that listening closer or harder helps.
It doesn't.
It just exposes me to this harsh reality:
 I can't hear you the way I want to,

and all of us deserve to be heard. Even my father,
who never knew what I sounded like,
or if words were merely patterns of dreams.

IV.

I Keep Weaving Surprises into a Shoreline

I cannot piece together silence
once a blue heron shivers a fish until it's dead.
I can only witness that shaking in solitude,
because I have arrived too late,
like I did as a field medic, too late
to save everyone.

The heron shocks a fish into submission,
into its beak, hallowed with death.
Although the fish makes no common sound,
I hear men begging for a quick, clean death.
As a field medic, I moved liquid from body
to gasping body, as thoughtless
and numbed to death, touching threads
between life and uncertain death.

During a battle, I'd go into that terrible silence,
moving through bullets
with eternal patience of a heron
studying a slivery fish.

I'd stitch sound to sorrow. Carry hope
as a limp body, place pressure on wounds,
stanch endless bleeding. I was often too late,
a reoccurring nightmare. I am late
to save the fish. I'm too late to save silence.

Nature drives instinct. Nature shapes silence,
divides it into moments before and after violence.
Death either ripples or lingers. I was too late
to apply rescue breathing, crack ribs,
crunching them like fish bones.

Breath to breath, breath to breath. If I failed,
I would add to the eternal silence,
until death became an afterthought,
as casual as a heron swallowing a fish

I must testify. I must hauntingly witness.
I must shake this silence awake.

How long will it be before the heron takes off,
lands, nests? How far from shore to quiet shore?
When will life settle down?

88

My Memory Keeps Naming the Dead

            I tear apart
    a fallen brown beech leaf,
               my sacrifice to grief.

God created both sacrifice and sadness.

I wish I could lie
and say   my heart doesn't bruise;
     but it does.

My heart shimmers with awakenings
of love: love gone,
love taken away.
                  God forgiven
o   r God forgotten?   Which?

At night, on a beech branch, no color
stands out against this moody landscape.
            What do I want to know,
except how to extend love?
       I want to be grateful for love
           and how long it lasted.
I can't.
       I can only feel tremendous loss,
while asking God
          why death?

I keep tearing that fallen beech tree leaf
         because
it contains knowledge of someone's death.

         Love and loss
are both recognizable by their shape.
       God forgotten
or God forsaken?
         God doesn't say.

So, too, a beech leaf doesn't say.
      I hear it suffer with its pain
of being torn into shreds.

Its trail of leaf fragments
            looks like tears,

a night without stars,
a wailing no one can stop.

            This beech leaf cries
as I rip
        and tear,
                rip
                    and tear.

        I hear its agony.

God created pain and brokenness.

I needed to find a release for my grief,
and unfortunately, I plucked this beech leaf,
        made it into an unwilling victim,
and I hear its agony.

        It sounds like me.

God created moans and pleas.

I cannot piece together that leaf I've ripped apart.

            It wasn't fair to that beech leaf.

God created a beech tree,   its leaf,
                    Nature's fact leaves fall
        and are replaced next season.

        Sometimes, we act without thinking.
Sometimes, we do not know how to handle grief.

I never thought to ask that leaf,
            never thought it was alive,
        never asked God for permission
        to tear apart that leaf.

Right now, I'm asking this beech leaf to forgive me.

Forgiveness or forgetfulness?
Which?

I think there remains one truth, at least,
        to ease hearts of loss —

another morning will rise,
a red glow,
        like a cardinal perched on this horizon,
and everywhere
will appear   differently
with a new perspective on life and love
and death.

I search for fingerprints on a torn beech leaf
to see if God had a hand in creating death.

I only find green stains on my fingertips.

        Remains of my pain.

    Your memory.

        A graveyard distance from grief.

A wind full of emptiness asks:
                        What remains?

Snow Weaves Aimlessly Across Pastures as Sheep

1.

I'm weaving on a loom in a meditative state:
          What is *careful*?

Certainly, float-pattern of sheep
in restive distance,
                    their unnamed feeling
when in afternoon light grazing,
                         unaware I am nearby,
          watching over them
          as subtle as a single cloud.

Surely,
          first tentative snow,
          that color of sheared wool,
my bewilderment
                    as a child as it lazily wafted,
filtering out pines
          and tamaracks in the obliteration.
That might be harmless.
                    Or, perhaps, the way winter
wind bleats.   Or, maybe,
          light on my arms.
                                        Or calm.

When I never know what to say,
                         avoiding harmful words,
questions melt on my tongue trying to keep my words
tightly locked inside me.
          I toss away the key, zip shut.

I am definitely careful when I shear sheep,
clipping away silence,
                         tugging loose wool.
Is this *tenderness*?
          This snow? Or a hush-a-by
in those pines? Or that uncertain light
                    taken by curtains

of a momentary blizzard?
          Or spinning wool into thread?

I listen for desire inside
these moments,   those familiar rote-routines
          where distance becomes relative.
               Clipping wool,
letting it fall;
               snow grazing fields,
meandering closer.
                    My blood flows with tree sap.

          I keep trimming.
          I keep weaving.   I keep herding
silence across those *Calming-Down Pastures*
in *Snowfall*
          of Intention and Attention-to-Detail.

I ease my way through barn's half-light,
          through weaving   and interweaving
of soft-spoken days,
               long footfalls to my bedroom
and white, down-filled coverlets.

I need to stop my consciousness.
               Let my questioning ways
glide quietly over pine needles off a branch
splayed on the ground, softening my movement
          as I pull apart my aches
               like carding the wool.

               I spin wool into thread,
as it speaks about snow,
          feeling it sliding
          between my two fingers, caressing
               its absence, its absolute presence.

2.

I no longer question what happens next in life,
what gets assigned importance for memory,
what time clips away.   *Caring* means *letting go*.

I no longer wonder what will touch me deeply,
what stage of brokenness needs repair,
constellations continuously spiral in endless space

      without asking *why* they are held
          but trusting in gravity, not challenging
delicate moments   or their fragile ways.

      I've used a skiff to cross the *Lake of Doubt*.
Navigating by sextant and stars, trusting my skill.
      Whether or not there were waves, I held fast.

I'm thinking about my acceptance of how delicately I've aged,
how my body drifts, following the coastline of Acceptance.
      I let my hands leave the boat's tiller and untie the anchor.

      As I relax, I visualize
         all the beauty I've seen
and those multitude of surprises I've learned in life.

Herding sheep taught me to watch without being seen,
      how to fade into this world. Snow teaches waiting,
      glancing as it speeds by,   leaving me behind.

      Working on a loom told me to focus on making
our world into a sensible gift. Mapping star formations
      allows me to know silence and consistency.

I sit,   quilt-making   with these pieces
      cut from the past,   what fades, what takes
new shape. Let my quilt warm you on a long winter night.

3.

      Let me brushstroke this world into quiet,
distill my visions during silent meditation,
      the same noiselessness concentration of sheep
      nudging grass in *The Promising-Fields*.

            When I focus,
I find little difference between that grass-munching

and sunlight reflecting off fallen snow.

        This can be such a slight-breath world,
with same intention as Chinese quick-brush painting,
    or pine needles falling to soften ground,
or unchecked snow,   or a sail unfurling wind.

    This can be a hardly-noticed-silent-world.

Those Chinese paintings allow mistakes:
some include mistakes on purpose, their intention,
their proof of imperfect moments,
    this imperfect world,
    imperfect me.   This world smears,
blends, contains blank moments of nothing happening.

      I must trust how my mind wanders,
finds amazement,   counting my good days
as sheep   or snowflakes   or dizzying stars.

How harmless
    to just not focus on chores or needs!
  Same as skimming a lake in my boat,
  never docking,
    never considering returning.

I keep emptying my mind,
  painting,   or writing haiku,
ignoring grammar, sense, reason, or linear thought
without pattern,
    sheep searching for tender grass,
  or those many shapes of snowflakes.

Did I start to write about grief?   Or resurrection?
I shall become as plain-spoke as my Amish grandfather.
  I shall say my mind,   minding what I say.

4.

Today, I tend sheep,
  being tender with them,
bringing them back safely,

removing their heavy wool
before the sun becomes too hot.

                      My sheep accept me
and the clippers.
          They hold stillness, as still as trees
or calm water.
                      They hold their silhouettes,
not wavering,   uncertain shadows.

              They have no complaints,
and are compliant.
          I snip   and tug. This tender work
takes steady hands,
          a quiet heart,   a relaxed mind.
One might say *mindful*.

              I scrub off dirt and card wool,
purposefully making it into thread.
                      I don't speak.

    I hum a calm-down restful tune,
                  tuneless and made-up on the spot.
I spin words and act reassuringly,
          images,   brushstrokes
filled with quiet of snow, water, pine needles.
          I add this concentration to my weaving.
I shuttle and tighten.
          Fabric snaps.   I repeat.

Sheep rest now.
                  Stars make no noise.
    This day floats into night.
I finish my own making, unmaking,
          trimming, tightening,
letting thread sift through my fingers.

              I bring this to you:
a quilt to snuggle under in coldest winter.

5.

When I work on the handloom
        or write in partial light, I dream
of designs, their inevitable imperfections,

how I have to accept mistakes in order to learn.
        I make delicate choices, a drifting sailboat
on waves of doubt, allowing life to happen.

        Life spirals, galaxies or leaves falling.

                What is harmless?
Even brushstrokes make tension
and release.   And, this meditation began
about *careful memory*,
        then, maybe, *grief*; or *recovery*.

                But words scurry
as thousands of blown snowflakes.
        I think: *introspection.*
Or, *inevitable questions.*

I have no easy answers.   None I can focus on.
        Words draw up their anchors.

                No,
        maybe this process includes *stillness*,
                or *caregiving.*

This difficult process equals sheering sheep: the tug.

        I follow footfall of heartbeats
from squeaking wood as my house settles into itself.
        I brushstroke sheep, star charts,
                snow off the porch.

My mind clutters.   I am not *mind-full* or calm
        in surprises of what is harmless.

        I attend, a night-watcher,
while my wife lets sleep fall as snowflakes.

6.

This should be a *care-full* world
full of caring,
            instead of a *care-less* one
            with careless words and actions.

I prefer the way sheep move tenderly,
nibbling calming springtime grasses
            without a care in the world,
                    nodding their heads
                    as if silently praying,
trusting I will treat them kindly.

            I spin their wool into threads of a story,
while snow grazes across the sky.

7.

I'm weaving on a loom in a meditative state:
            what is *careful*?

                        The gentle music of love.
            The world meditates on that melody.

Love grazes in the fields of our hearts,
and weaves us together into a pattern.

                The same way snow hushes us
as we stare into its calm patterns of snowflakes.

            How careful I must be to touch you,
as if spinning wool
                        into noiseless thread.

            How careless of me
to forget to tell you   I love you.

I shuttle the loom to tighten the fabric of love.

            I do this work without thinking.
It became as natural as dreaming.

Rowing on a Lake

Encircled by leaves twisting each season, I row
into a lake's center, to be surrounded by quietness.
Raising oars, letting drips ease into a rim of pine shadows,
my hands are rubbed raw from rowing
against the grain of water. My fingers let go.
Let go into this flow of silence. Let go into flow
of loons' swooning. My breath slips
into ease. I release problems and tension from my body
like tossing an anchor into this lake. My concerns
scatter sea gulls. Anguish falls as leaves
onto the reflection about my life's choices.
Every moment smears.

There will be calmness and solemness,
trusting water's slow, calm movement
to get to where I need to be next.
And where will I need to be? I don't know;
don't care. I must trust where I end up next.

A loon moans about its search for love,
its never-ending desire, its intense loneliness.
This world contains uncertainty. Its pulse rate
needs to slow down, take intentional steps,
be tentative about making rash decisions,
seeking love among shadows of tree lines on water.

I did not need to row onto a lake to find love
or silence or introspection
or find whatever I needed to discover.
I just needed to listen deeply inside myself.

I don't have to row back to where I began.
I could choose to follow the loon's distress signal
bouncing off hills and trees.
I can take my time before going anywhere,
before dipping my oars and pulling against water.
Time really doesn't matter.
Silence waits for everyone.

Acknowledgments

I want to thank the following magazines for publishing these poems, and many of these poems have been changed over time.

Atticus Review: "I Call This "Dipping Hands in Water to Feel How the World Moves""

Autumn Sky Poetry Daily: "Phone Call," "Sonata," "Sounds I Cannot Hear Clearly Anymore Add Up to the Sum of Silence"

Bitterzoet: "Listening to a Meadowlark," "Summertime and Living Was Not Easy"

Blue Nib: "Escaping the Labyrinth," "What They Never Tell You About Growing Up"

Bollman Bridge Review: "Snow Weaves Aimlessly Across Pastures as Sheep"

Broadkill River Review: "Occupation of Hands," "Son, My Chronology Ends with You"

Comstock Review: "Elegy," "In the Storm," "Universal Sign for Silence is a Hush Finger to Lips," "Suddenness Flies in Swiftly and Exits Extremely Slowly"

Connecticut Poetry Review: "Summer of My Seventh Year"

Gyroscope: "The Shirt"

January: "The Day is Speechlessly Broken," "My Father in a Noise-Filled World"

Kentucky Review: "Letter to My Son"

Loch Raven Review: "Message Was Delivered"

Meadowlark Review: "Memorial Tree"

Mental Health Journal: "The Grief Counselor," "Hearing

Indirectly My Son Needs Drug Rehab"

Muddy River Review: "Unfinished"

Night Garden: "A Great Length"

Nine Mile Magazine: "The Mockingbird Mimics the Out-of-Tune Grand Pianos in the Extravagant Neighborhoods"

One Art Magazine: "Emptying Time," "I Had Been Expecting This Phone Call Since January," "Lastness of Silence," "Manifestation," "Story of Absence," "Talking to My Brother"

Poppy Road Review: "A River Rushing By"

Red Wolf Review (flyer): "Sign Language with the Watery Movement of Hands"

Seven Circles Press: "Learning the Hard Way"

Shanti Arts Quarterly: "Hot Chocolate"

Silver Birch Press: "Hiding Place, a Place of Riddles," "My Mother's *Forever* House"

Storyteller Poetry Review: "Fishing with My Son," "Gifts My Father Gave Me," "How Death Works"

Sheila-Na-Gig: "Calculus of Love"

Thimble Lit Magazine: "Deafness in the Silent Language"

Writers Tribe Review (theme: Family): "How My Six-Year-Old Son Learned Counting"

"A Horizon is Vague at a Distance" won the *Editor's Choice* for the *Rattle Ekphrastic Contest, December, 2020*

"A Horizon is Vague at a Distance" was republished as a *Rattle Magazine* as a *Daily Poem by Email* (January 7, 2024)

"Champions of the World" was selected as *Featured Poet,* for the

Aurorean (Fall/Winter 2019–2020)

"Phone Call" (originally "Boats Sailing in Uncharted Territory") was nominated for a *Pushcart Award* by *Autumn Sky Poetry Daily*, 2021

"The Shirt" was a video produced and narrated by Patty Mooney (Crystal Pyramid Productions, 2023)

"Symphony of Quiet" appeared in a forthcoming, unnamed anthology

"Sounds I Cannot Hear Clearly Anymore Add Up to the Sum of Silence" was nominated for a *Pushcart Award* by *Autumn Sky Poetry Daily*, 2023

"Traveling through Life with My Son" (appeared as "My Son in the Back Seat Asks the Eternal Question,") in the "Center Stage" feature in *The Wild Word Magazine*

About the Author

Martin Willitts Jr is a retired Librarian that trained Librarians for New York State Public Libraries. He lives in Syracuse, New York. He is an editor for Comstock Review, and he is the judge for the New York State Fair Poetry Competition.

He won 2014 Dylan Thomas International Poetry Contest; Stephen A. DiBiase Poetry Prize, 2018; Editor's Choice, Rattle Ekphrastic Challenge, December 2020; 17th Annual Sejong Writing Competition, 2022; and the 2025 Silent River Poetry Prize. His 27 full-length collections include the National Ecological Award winner for "Searching for What You Cannot See" (Hiraeth Press, 2013) and the Blue Light Award 2019, "The Temporary World". His recent books are "Ethereal Flowers" (Shanti Arts Press, 2023); "Rain Followed Me Home" (Glass Lyre Press, 2023); "Leaving Nothing Behind" (Fernwood Press, 2023); "The Thirty-Six Views of Mount Fuji" (Shanti Arts Press, 2024); "All Beautiful Things Need Not Fly" (Silver Bowl Press, 2024); "Martin Willitts Jr: Selected Poems" (FutureCycle Press, 2024); "Love Never Cools When It Is Hot" (Red Wolf Editions, 2025); 2025 Silent River Poetry Prize, "One Thousand Origami Paper Cranes Fly Away in Search of Peace."

Website: https://nyq.org/poets/poet/martin-willitts
Instagram: @mwillitts01
Facebook: martin.j.willitts